©2014 AKANSON Media Group, LLC
All Rights Reserved.

Table of Contents

Preface..vii

The Amazing World of Interviews

   Types of Interviews.. 2

      -The Four Main Types of Interviews

      -Telephone Interviews

      -Group Projects

      -Simulations

      -Pre-employment Testing

      -Lunch/ Dinner Interviews

      -Behavioral Interviewing

      -How to Prepare for a Behavioral Interview?

      -Ability & Aptitude Tests

      -Personality Tests & Motivation Questionnaires

Well, that caught me off guard

   Preparation 11

      -Preparing for the Interview—What to Expect

      -The Basic Materials

      -Analyze the Position

      -Set Your Objective

      -Research the Organization

      -Sources of Information

      -Put Yourself in the Interviewer's Shoes

      -What Worries Interviewers?

      -Prepare Your Own Case

      -Be Prepared for the Interview

      -Internal Applicants

Procedures, Procedures, and More Procedures

   The Interview Process 24

      -The Format

      -Responding Positively

      -The Second Interview

      -Waiting

      -Making an Exit

      -Saying Thank You

      -The Offer Letter

Uh, could you repeat the question?
General Interview Questions 29
- *General Information*
- *Educational Background*
- *Work History*
- *Career Interests*
- *Skills*
- *Motivation*
- *Illegal Questions*
- *Ethical Principles of College Recruiting For Candidates*
- *Questions For The Candidate To Ask The Employer*
- *Do Not Ask The Following*
- *Types of Questions*
- *Why Has This Vacancy Arisen?*
- *Do You Promote Internally Where Possible?*
- *What Opportunities Do You Offer To Gain Extra-Training, Qualifications, or Experience?*
- *If I Was Offered This Job, Where Would You See Me In Five Years?*
- *Where Does The Company Aim To Be In Five Years?*
- *When Can I Expect To Hear From You?*

The Art of Interviewing 31
- *Practice Makes Perfect*
- *Interview Attire: * Men * Women*
- *Essential Qualities*
- *Making a Good First Impression*
- *During an Interview Projecting the Right Image*
- *Interview Tips*
- *Market your Skills*
- *Would you like a Drink?*
- *Taking Notes*
- *– What do you think the role of a (whatever the job is)?*
- *What do you know about our company*
- *Tell me about yourself.*
- *Sell me this pen.*
- *Tell me a story.*
- *Why do you want this job?*
- *Why do you want to leave your present job?*
- *What do you feel you can bring to this job?*
- *What are your greatest strengths?*
- *What is your biggest weakness?*

- How would your colleagues describe you?
- How would your friends describe you?
- What would your boss say about you?
- Where do you see yourself in five years?
- How long do you expect to stay with this company?
- How long would it take you to make a useful contribution to this company?
- What motivates you?
- How do you approach a typical project?
- What do you enjoy most in your current job?
- How well do you take direction?
- How do you handle criticism?
- Describe a situation in which your work was criticized.
- What is the biggest challenge you have faced at work?
- Do you enjoy routine tasks?
- How do you operate under stress?
- What do you dislike most at work?
- What were your most significant achievements in your present job?
- If you could start again, what career decisions would you make differently?
- Do you consider that your career so far has been a success?
- How does this job fit into your career plans?
- What appeals least to you about this job?
- Describe a situation which, in hindsight you could have handled better.
- What sort of decisions do you find difficult to make?
- What sort of people do you find difficult to work with?
- What is your present boss like?
- What is your present boss greatest weakness?
- Why have you been with your present employer so long?
- Why have you been with your employer for such a short time?
- How do you evaluate your present company?
- You look like a job jumper to me.
- Why haven't you found a new job yet?
- How can you attend this interview while you are still employed somewhere else?
- Are you talking to other organizations as well as us?
- What other types of job or organizations are you applying to?
- You may be overqualified for this job.
- Reassuring the Interviewer
- What do you think about any subject of current affairs or events?
- What do you think are the key trends in this industry?
- What is your management style?

- *Are you a good manager?*
- *Are you a natural leader?*
- *How do you work in a team?*
- *How do you get the best from people?*
- *How do you resolve conflict in your team?*
- *What outside interest do you have?*
- *What have you read and enjoyed lately?*
- *How creative are you?*
- *What is your present salary?*
- *What salary are you expecting?*
- *How much do you think you are worth?*
- *When would you expect a promotion?*
- *Salary Variables*
- *Deal Negotiating*
- *DON'T GIVE AWAY FREE CONCESSIONS*
- *Get All Your Cards on the Table – Get Any Skeletons Out In The Open*
- *Bad Timing*

Interviewing at Institutions of Higher Learning.. 51

Final Thoughts 54

Preface

This book took me one year to write. During that time, I applied to countless jobs in the government and private sector. Each application was strong; however, I was not selected for an interview. I could go into the many reasons why this happened, or I could tell you the blessing in all this . . . the reason for my joy . . . and it is because the Lord had a better path for me. It is a path not for the faint-hearted. A path often pondered, but not ventured: I own a business.

I wrote this book understanding that if I landed an interview, I would be selected for the position, and that's any position, for which I interviewed. Why? Because there are time-tested strategies that set me apart from other interviewees. This is what I share with you in this handy manual. I've had jobs in sales and won an internship with the federal government. For each interview, whether it was for the jobs I had in sales, the customers to whom I sell products, or the internship I won with the federal government during college, I used these techniques and methods to prepare.

It is my hope that you find this book to be a treasure trove of information that really works when put into practice. I like to help motivated job-seekers sharpen their resumes and prepare for interviews. Feel free to get in touch with me, should you need one-on-one coaching! Enjoy . . .

Somewhere in New Jersey, August 3, 2014

Phil Koffi
Principal and Owner of AKANSON Media Group, LLC

in·ter·view *noun* \ˈin-tər-ˌvyü\

An interview is a formal meeting in which one or more people question, consult, or evaluate another person. Example: a job interview.

Types of Interviews

Telephone Interviews

In an effort to save time and money, some employers will conduct screening interviews by phone. Since you may expect calls from employers at any time, it is important for you to have a reliable answering machine or voice mail with a professional message; employers are not usually entertained by quirky messages or long music interludes.

Many job candidates find telephone interviews more difficult than personal interviews because the interviewee will typically not receive any nonverbal feedback to help gauge responses. You should prepare for the telephone interview with the same diligence as you would for a person-to-person interview.

Below are some tips to help you prepare for a telephone interview:

- When the secretary or interviewer calls to arrange the telephone interview, be sure to ask for basic information if it is not offered: who will conduct the interview, name and title (ask for spelling of name if you are unsure; again, this information is valuable for your follow-up) and ask for the projected length of the interview so that you may make appropriate arrangements.
- As you prepare for the interview, make sure your room is void of noise and other distractions. Try to sit at a desk or table with your resume in front of you for easy reference. Good posture will help you project a professional tone on the telephone.
- You should also keep a note pad and pen nearby to jot down any ideas or questions that may come to mind.
- Arrange to interview in a comfortable place, where you will not easily be distracted.
- When introductions are made, write down the names of those who will participate in the interview with you and acknowledge each of the interviewers by name.
- If a formal or long question is asked, it may be helpful for you to write down key words or aspects of the question to be sure you answer all of the parts of the question that was asked.
- Think about the question and your response before answering. If you need to consider your response before answering, let the committee or interviewer know that you are thinking about the question so they will understand the brief silence from your end.
- Answer the questions fully, but do not ramble on after you have given your answer. It is common that interviewers will be silent after your response as they consider the next question to ask. Do not allow their silence to prompt you to extend your answer. To signal you are through answering, it is a good idea to summarize your response.
- Again, be prepared with questions and end your interview with a statement expressing your interest in the position.
- Be sure to thank the interviewers for their time at the closing of the interview and that you look forward to speak with them again soon.
- Follow-up with a thank you letter within 24 hours after the telephone interview. If multiple individuals participated in the telephone interview, it is best to write thank you letters to each interviewer.

Panel Interviews

As a time-management method, some organizations will arrange panel interviews. You may be interviewing with as many as five or six employers at one time. This can be a very intimidating situation. Try to establish rapport with each person through eye contact. Whenever possible, try to incorporate their names in your responses.

Group Projects

If an organization intends to hire a large training class, a group project may be a part of the interview process. The group project is used to see how potential employees would work together to solve a situation or problem. Managers or human resource personnel will be present to evaluate individual contributions to the group project. The evaluators will look for assertiveness, analytical abilities, communication skills, and the ability to involve others in solving the situation.

Simulations

In an effort to determine how you would respond to typical job responsibilities, an employer may engage you in role play or other simulations. For example, if you were applying for a position in sales, the interviewer may pick up a paper clip from the desk and ask you to "Sell this paper clip to me." Other simulation projects may include reading through a scenario and responding, in writing, your course of action to the situation.

Pre-employment Testing

Some employers use personality tests and tests of knowledge as part of their interview process. As with any test, be sure to read all instructions carefully before you begin.

Lunch/Dinner Interviews

Your interview schedule may include a lunch or dinner meeting. Even though this may seem like a more relaxed and social time, remember that you are still being evaluated. Conversation should be your major concern, not the food. Always wait for the employer to open their menu as your cue to explore the menu. Often, the employer may talk with you for 10-15 minutes before ever considering the menu. Always follow the employer's lead. Spend only a few minutes looking at the menu; choose something that is easy to eat and familiar to you, this is not a good time to try something new. Take small bites of your food so that you are always prepared to answer the employer's questions.

Behavioral interviewing is based on the premise that the best way to predict future behavior is to determine past behavior. If you have experience with traditional interviews, you will find behavioral interviewing different in several ways:

- Instead of asking how you would behave in a particular situation, the interviewer will ask how you did behave.
- Expect the interviewer to question and probe your behavior in a situation. Depending on your viewpoint, you may view the interview as a therapy session or an interrogation!
- The interviewer will ask you to provide details, and will not allow you to theorize or generalize about several events.
- The interview will be a more structured process that will concentrate on areas important to the interviewer, rather than allowing you to concentrate on areas that you may feel are important.
- You may not get a chance to deliver any prepared stories.
- Most interviewers will take detailed notes throughout the interview.

The behavioral interviewer has been trained to objectively collect and evaluate information, and works from a profile of desired behaviors that are needed for success on the job. Because the behaviors a candidate has demonstrated in previous positions are likely to be repeated, you will be asked to share situations in which you may or may not have exhibited these behaviors. Your answers will be tested for accuracy and consistency.

If you are an entry-level candidate with no previous related experience, the interviewer will look for behaviors in situations similar to those of the target position:

- Describe a major problem you have faced and how you dealt with it.
- Give an example of when you had to work with a team to accomplish a task or project.
- What class did you like most? What did you like about it?

Follow-up questions will test for consistency and determine if you exhibited the desired behavior in that situation:

- Can you give me an example?
- What did you do?
- What did you say?
- What were you thinking?
- How did you feel?
- What was your role?
- What was the result?

You will notice an absence of questions such as, "Tell me about yourself."

How to Prepare for a Behavioral Interview

- ✓ Recall recent situations that show favorable behaviors or actions, especially involving coursework, work experience, leadership, teamwork, initiative, planning, and customer service.
- ✓ Prepare short descriptions of each situation. Be ready to give details if asked.

During a Behavioral Interview

- Use the STAR (situation, task, action, and result) storytelling technique.
- Be sure the result reflects positively on you.
- Be honest. Don't embellish or omit any part of the story. The interviewer will find out if your story is built upon a weak foundation.

- Be specific. Don't generalize about several events. Give a detailed accounting of each event.

- Do not be threatened or anxious about a behavioral interview. Keep in mind the behavioral interviewer is looking for past actions only.
- Adopt a similar tone to the interviewer. If they are very formal you need to follow suit. Be very wary of anything more than gentle humor unless your interviewer is injecting a lot of humor into the conversation (in which case you can laugh politely at their jokes – don't burst into loud screaming laughter).
- Don't ask your interviewer questions about salary, holiday, sick pay etc. If you do this it looks as if you are only interested in the job for the money. If they offer you the job you can discuss this later.

You will often find yourself in a one – to – one interview, very probably with the person who will be your direct manager if you get the job. But of course, that's not the only type of interview there is. Here are some other kinds of interviews you may come across:

Panel Interview

You may find yourself being interviewed by three or four people. This might include the line manager for the job, someone from personnel, perhaps a technical person if you are applying for a technical position, maybe even a union representative or a psychologist. Panel interviews tend, by their nature, to be more formal than some one – to – one interviews. This makes them more daunting and stressful, but there's no reason why they should be any harder to handle than any other interview. You should know in advance that a panel would interview you. Try to find their names – if you didn't realize that you were being interviewed by a panel until your arrival ask the receptionist for their names and write them down.

Remember the following:

- Shake hands with everyone on the panel. If it happens to be a large panel – more than about half a dozen – your alternative is to make a spot decision as you walk in that you will shake hands only with the chairperson (the one who stands and greets you), unless of course others offer you their hand.
- Make eye contact with everyone on the panel and make sure all feel included in your answers.
- Give the bulk of your attention to the person who asked the question you are answering.

When you come to ask questions of your own, direct them primarily at the person who is chairing the interview.

Sequential Interview

This is far more common in large organizations. You may find yourself in a series of one–on–one interviews with different people – maybe the line manager for the job, a more senior manager, a personnel representative or maybe a technical person. Apart from the danger of feeling that you are running a mental marathon, this is quite a good system for you. You get to start each interview fresh, so even if you feel you under performed at the last one, you can still give a stunning performance at the next.

The interviewers, of course, are not operating in isolation. They will have discussed in advance what areas each will cover and they will compare notes at the end before reaching a decision. They may also talk to each other between interviews. If this happens, you may find yourself being questioned about something you've already covered with the previous interviewer – very possibly they have asked the next person to probe the same area. With sequential interviews, you need to bear in mind that each interviewer is looking at a different aspect of your application. There's no point in them all repeating the same exercise with you.

Ability and Aptitude Tests

Tests such as these measure your specific skills and give a score, which tells your potential employer what your level of ability is, or what your potential for learning new skills is. Research has shown that ability and aptitude tests are an excellent guide to future performance and it's therefore no surprise that employers are using them more frequently.

These tests aren't general knowledge tests they are aimed at assessing your ability to reason or think in a logical manner. Some of these tests are broad in scope but others focus on verbal skills and numeric, these being the most popular.

Ability and aptitude tests are a bit like taking exams. There is a given time period to complete them and they are often in the form of multiple choice. Generally, they become more difficult as the test goes on and sometimes there may be more questions than you can answer. This isn't important it's the proportion of answers you get right not the number of questions you complete.

So how important are ability and aptitude tests in relation to the rest of the recruitment process? You can get a good idea of when in the selection process the test takes place. The earlier you take it the more important generally it is. If it is the very first thing you do – even before attending an interview – it is probably being used as a screening process and you will only be invited for an interview should you reach a certain score. The later in the process that you take the test the more likely it is that it will be treated as one of only many parts of the selection process.

Preparing for Aptitude and Ability Tests

You have seen that it's useful to practice for these tests by getting hold of sample questions or practice papers but what else can you do? Here are a few tips;

- ✓ Practice not only with test papers but also with other related exercises such as brainteasers and puzzles (you can get these in your local newsagents).
- ✓ For aptitude tests in particular, play word games and mathematical puzzles.
- ✓ Practice your mental arithmetic and things like long division and multiplication.

- ✓ For a numeric test, find out if you'll be allowed to take a calculator into the test. If so, remind yourself (if necessary) of how to use a calculator to work out such things as percentages.

If you've been asked to take any aptitude or ability tests you'll want to practice as we have already advised you – so make sure you do!

Personality Tests and Motivation Questionnaires

These tests are very different from ability and aptitude tests because there are no right or wrong answers and the tests are not generally timed. They simply aim to assess what kind of person you are. The point of this is to see how suited you are to the type of work you will do, how well you would fit into the company culture and how well you would get with the team you would form part of.

Since you have no idea what the company is looking for in terms of personality type there's no point in giving anything but truthful answer to these questions. These tests benefit you as much as the employer. If you really don't fit in with the corporate culture or the type of work, you'd be doing you probably wouldn't want the job anyway. The kind of thing these tests will identify include:

- ➤ *What motivates you*
- ➤ *Your attitude to life and work*
- ➤ *How you relate to other people*
- ➤ *How you handle emotions*
- ➤ *How you approach problems*

Motivation questionnaires are similar to personality tests but they focus specifically on what drives you, how long you maintain your energy levels for a particular task, what situations tend to motivate you more or less and so on. They are more often than not used for staff development (once you are in the job), than for recruitment, you may however encounter them during a selection process.

Assessment centers are another of the tools employers sometimes use – alongside interviews and psychometric tests – to assess potential candidates. They are really another form of test, but this time on a more practical level. You undertake some kind of exercise, or perhaps several, such as group discussion exercises, role-plays or team project exercises. (If you are also taking psychometric tests these make take place at the assessment center). An assessor or team of assessors will observe you during the exercise.

Just like ability and aptitude testing, assessment centers are one of the most accurate predictors of future performance. They are also said to be a fair and objective way of assessing candidates. The point here is that if you really are the best person for the job you can be confident and it will show.

There are several types of exercise you might be asked to perform. The key thing to remember is that even when the exercise is geared towards an end result, such as making a decision, the way you carry out the exercise will generally be at least as important as your final result. This means that you should make sure: 1) the assessors can see what preparation you have done by making notes where appropriate; and, 2) you indicate how you have arrived at any conclusions.

There are countless assessment center exercises you might be asked to do, but here is a quick guide to the main types you may encounter:

In Tray—This is just what it sounds like. You're given the hypothetical in tray of the person whose job you would be taking over. You have to go through everything in it and mark on each piece of correspondence how you would handle it and what action you would take arising from it. Since these annotations are all the assessors have to go on, you need to make sure you mark down anything, which might be useful or relevant.

Case Study—Here, you are given plenty of factual information about a business issue on which you have to make a decision. The information may be unclear in places. You have to assess the information and arrive at a decision, which you then relay to the assessors either in a brief written report or as a short presentation. Although it is important to make a decision if you are briefed to do so, your approach to the issue is as important as your conclusion.

Group Discussion—This is very similar to the case study except that you have to make a decision or recommendation – or perhaps several – in a group together with other candidates. Sometimes you are each given a particular role to play but you may all be given the same information.

Interview Role Play—In this exercise you are given a brief on a meeting you are about to have with a role player. You should use the brief to plan the meeting – the way you do this will be a significant part of the overall assessment. (You'll be given anything up to 30 minutes to prepare.) The meeting, as your brief will tell you, will involve either discussing an issue with the role player, or using them to help you collect information about the issue. Either way, you will be expected to use the information, or the results of the discussion, to reach a decision on the issue.

Team Tests

If an employer is particularly keen to know how you will fit into a team, they may ask you to take part in some kind of team test. This kind of test generally lasts all-day or even over a couple of days. It might involve anything from hiking across the moors to building a model of the empire state building out of matches. You will be observed and assessed throughout the test.

One positive point to bear in mind here is that these tests cost a lot of money and the prospective employer would not spend this kind of money if they thought the job didn't warrant it and the investment was worthwhile. So, the fact that you've been asked to participate in this test alone should boost your confidence.

Unless you're applying for a job as an out-of-bounds manager, it's highly unlikely that your prospective employer gives will care as to whether you are any good at hiking across the

It's fairly unlikely that they really want to see how good your model of the empire state building made out of matches is either! What is really going on here is your prospective employer wants to see how well you work as part of a team. It's impossible to spend the time pretending to be someone that you are not and, in any case, would you want a job on this basis. This type of test is likely to put you under enough pressure and you would have a hard time putting on an act for the whole duration even if you wanted to.

So, you must be aware that it's your team performance that counts, not the project you've been given. Try and be yourself but avoid extremes, which may deter the assessors from recommending you:

- Don't take over officiously and become too bossy (although if the team genuinely defers to you as its leader that's fine).
- Don't be as reserved as a field mouse that you seem like you are not involved. Make sure you make enough of a contribution to be assessed on.
- Don't get into arguments with other team members. If conflict arises play a diplomatic role, it will show you in a much better light to your assessor.
- Don't try to be smart and say, *"What's the point in building a model out of match sticks anyway?"*
- If there are other teams competing with yours it's a good idea to show your competitive streak, but not to the point of ruthlessness. Try and adopt the approach of "It's only a game, but all things being equal we'd like to win and we'll give it our best shot." You aren't likely to get the job just because your team wins but it is how you play the game that counts

Apart from showing that you are the diplomat, the most useful roles you can take on in the team to impress your assessors are:

- Keep the team focused on the objective.
- Summarize how the team is doing from time to time.

Interviewers aren't in the business of holding second interviews just because they can't decide whom to offer the job to and they want to look at other candidates. The second interview is an opportunity to find out more about the candidates or to enable someone more senior to interview a shortlist of candidates. It may be that you were recruited through an agency that interviewed you initially so this might be the first time that you've actually met the employer.

Whatever the case it's not going to be a straight repeat of the first interview. You might find that you are asked to undergo psychometric tests, assessment center exercises or a technical interview alongside your second interview, which is all quite formal. On the other hand, an interview with a senior colleague or manager of your original interviewer can be quite informal, as they simply want to make sure that the first interviewer made an accurate assessment of you.

If there is an outstanding concern from your first interview it is not likely to be aired at a second interview. Your interviewers may be worried if you have significantly less experience than the other candidates or are very different from them in some other way. It may be that they are concerned that you are over qualified. Interviewers often throw one "wildcard" candidate into the shortlist and it could be you. So, they will need reassuring that you are the right applicant for the job and that any worrying features of your application are in fact strengths.

It is very possible that the interviewer at your second interview will put these concerns to you straight. If they don't, they will make it quite obvious where they need reassurance. Keep in mind that they called you back for a second interview so they obviously don't consider that your lack of experience (or whatever else bothers them) made you a non-starter. They obviously thought you had considerable strengths elsewhere to shortlist you despite their misgivings. They really do want to be reassured that you can do the job.

It's likely that you will be asked many questions directly related to your past performance at a second interview, some of these might be:

- *What improvements have you introduced in your current job?*
- *What have you done to increase productivity?*
- *What has been your biggest success?*
- *What has been your biggest mistake?*
- *How have you increased the profitability of your department?*

Should you have management experience you are also likely to be asked about this including questions such as whether you have done your own training, recruitment and so on. If the job is going to require you to relocate they are also likely to ask how you feel about this and whether your family will be in agreement.

Preparation

Once you have secured the interview, you should begin preparing. Do not think that you can simply walk into an interview and answer a few questions. The employer will often meet with several hundred candidates in order to find 5-7 potential employees. Your goal must be to demonstrate your interest and qualifications for the position. Preparation is key!

Interviewers have many expectations of you as a potential candidate for hire. You must know general information about the position for which you are interviewing. You must also be able to articulate your qualifications and interest. In addition, the employer expects you to have researched the organization and understands the nature of the business.

Many college seniors have not had the opportunity to participate in formal interviews; therefore, the process may seem intimidating and complex. However, through research and practice, interviewing skills can be perfected. It is a widely known fact that the best candidate does not always get the job. Many qualified candidates are passed over due to lack of interview preparation or an inability to articulate "fit" for the position. Once you arrive at the interview stage, it is your ability to sell yourself that will help ensure a job offer. The following suggestions outline proven methods of enhancing your interviewing skills and improving your opportunities of employment.

Preparing for the Interview – What to Expect

Congratulations!! You've got an interview. You must have impressed the interviewer with your resume and your application to get this far. They are not likely to interview every candidate, so clearly, they have already seen something in your application that stands out from the crowd. Of course, from your point of view, that probably seemed like the easy bit compared with the interview to come. But never fear once you know what you are doing winning the job you are applying for will be easy too!

The Basic Materials

Well at least your poor old interviewer doesn't have to make their choice completely blind. Even before they meet the prospective candidates, they have no less than four documents to help them make their decision. These fall into two categories: documents that help them define the job, and documents that help them assess the candidates. The documents that help them define the job are:

- The job description, which tells them the overall objective of the job and key responsibilities.
- The employee specification, which describes for them what skills and attributes the successful applicant will need to have.

You should have a copy of the job description, which is how you have assessed your ability to do the job! However, very few employers will show applicants the employee specification. You do have the other two pieces of paperwork, the ones which tell the interviewer what kind of person you are: 1) your resume; and, 2) your application form.

Your interviewer is trying to match up this pair of documents with the first – in other words they are trying to find the applicant who most closely matches the job requirements. Your job is to demonstrate that you are the one.

The interviewer – if they know anything at all about interviewing – will have two lists of questions to ask you:

- A list of questions to ask all candidates, which are questions about the job, which they draw up using the first two documents – the job description and the employee specification. Unless they ask you all the same questions, it's going to be almost impossible to assess which one of you best suits the job.
- Questions specifically for you, which they have formulated by looking through your application form and your resume. These might include questions about your own experience, skills, qualifications or circumstances and about your career, interests and working style.

Analyze the Position

Before you are able to convince an employer that you want to be a public relations specialist, it is important that you understand what a public relations specialist does. To gather this important information, you may start your research in the library. Current resources such as the <u>Occupational Outlook Handbook</u> and the work section of <u>Choices Planner</u> provide up-to-date information regarding job responsibilities, employment outlook, educational requirements, and starting salaries. This basic research will prove valuable as you prepare to demonstrate a match between your credentials and the position for which you are interviewing.

In addition, you are encouraged to do an internship in the field you wish to pursue. An internship will help you gain experience and provide you with firsthand knowledge of the field. Informational interviews provide another excellent source of gathering information on specific career fields.

Set Your Objective

An objective is a destination. If you don't know exactly where you are heading it's unlikely that you will get there efficiently. Or you may not get there at all. You might think that your objective is obvious – i.e. to get the job. Well you'd be right. And wrong. That tells you where you are going, but it doesn't tell you how you are going to get there. And just as a well-planned journey needs a route, as well as a destination, a well-planned objective must tell you not only where you are going but also how you are going to get there.

My objective is to get the job by demonstrating to the interviewer that I am the best person for it in terms of ability, experience and personality. And if you have any more information you can add in terms of the interviewer's specific priorities you can add this to your objective.

A clear well-conceived objective is a touchstone against which you can measure everything you do. It helps you stay focused. If any activity doesn't help you meet your objective, don't do it. Use the time for something that will further it. For example, you should research the organization to which you are applying. You need to do enough research to demonstrate that you have done your homework, but beyond that, what do you need to find out? You need to find out anything that helps meet your objective and nothing else.

Research the Organization

To begin, you must research the company or agency to determine the nature of the organization. The more you know about the employer, the more comfortable you will feel in the interview. A demonstrated knowledge of the organization will also help convince the interviewer of your interest. In order to prove genuine interest, many interviewers will begin the process with a question such as, "Why are you interested in our organization?" or "Tell me what you know about our company." This is certainly not a question that you can "bluff" your way through.

It is a mistake to assume that you know enough about the organization without conducting any research. Only through research will you be able to answer the question with confidence.

Through your research, you should become familiar with:

- type of organization and its function
- mission and goals
- products or services divisions and subsidiaries
- position description and career paths
- sales and earnings (if company is a public, for-profit organization)
- size
- competitors
- location, including international operations (if applicable)
- projects
- new trends in the field

Sources of Information

You can use a variety of resources to research organizations. Publicly held companies are easier to research for they are required by law to make certain information public. Privately held companies do not have the same requirements and are generally, more difficult to research. To begin, consider using the Internet to locate general information. There are several sites listed on the Career Related Web Sites page to help in researching companies. Also, consider articles from trade publications. The Career Services home page will provide links to many employment databases that will include company information. Annual reports and employment brochures also provide good information for beginning research.

- There are many directories available in the public libraries to help you in your research. Among the most popular are:
- Standard and Poor's Register of Corporations, Directors, and Executives
- Dun and Bradstreet's Guide to Your Investments
- Thomas' Register of American Manufacturers

- The Value Line Investment Survey
- Moody's

The public library has business periodicals and newspapers to help you research company trends and noteworthy ventures. The following publications are well-respected sources of information:

- The Wall Street Journal
- Business Week
- Forbes
- Fortune

Also, consider articles from trade publications, generally available through professional associations. If you are interviewing with a privately held company or agency, you will need to be more creative in your research approach. If you cannot find information using the recommended methods, try identifying employees or volunteers (for nonprofit agencies) to gather information; the Chamber of Commerce may also be able to provide limited information. You may also consider talking with employees of similar organizations to gain a general perspective of the industry.

Put Yourself in the Interviewer's Shoes

You need to know what the interviewer is looking for – why are they conducting these interviews? They have started with a pile of applications, which they have sifted through and narrowed down to the people who they are inviting for an interview, which includes you!

The interviewer isn't going to invite just anyone who they don't think can do the job so the list of interviewees will be made up entirely of people who, in their opinion, should be capable of doing the job. Once again, you should feel confident about this. You wouldn't be on the list unless the interviewer thought – on the basis of your application and resume – that you could do the job that they are advertising.

The interviewer has to decide which of the candidates is going to be most suitable for the job. They aren't trying to measure you against each other, but against the standards for the job itself. Either way, it's going to be a difficult choice for them. All the candidates will have strong and weak points, and the interviewer will have to weigh each of these up against each other. Do they want someone who has lengthy experience or would they rather go for someone with shorter but more relevant experience?

It's tough doing and interviewer's job. And it's tough for you too, because you know even less about what they are looking for than they do. However, even if you don't know what their priorities are, you know broadly what they are after. And if you know where your strengths and weaknesses are you can prepare to promote your strong points and find ways of making your week spots look less like weaknesses.

Prepare for the Expected

You can get ready for the interview by knowing what the interviewer is looking for, and making sure that you are ready to prove that you got it:

- Assess yourself for the job in the key areas of skills, experience and so on.
- Consider the key areas on your application form and RESUME that they are likely to ask you about.
- Think about whether your RESUME or application shows up anything, which might – rightly or wrongly – give your interviewer cause to worry about your ability to do the job.

It would be deeply unwise to walk into an important interview without doing any preparation in advance. The better prepared you are the better your chances at getting the job.

What Worries Interviewers?

These issues usually concern interviewers, so be prepared to answer:
- Lack of relevant experience.
- Lack of personal attributes, such as the ability to work under pressure or to motivate others.
- Slower progress up the career ladder than they would have expected.
- Employment gaps.

You may wonder about what you are supposed to do if the concern is founded. Suppose you really do lack the experience they need, or you did spend a year out of work because you couldn't get a job. In this case the most important thing to do is to be ready to answer the question. Look through your application and resume, and work out where the interviewer's concerns will lie. Then you can prepare answers to the questions.

In general, the best way to answer these questions when they are genuine is to be honest, but give plenty of compensating factors. If you genuinely lack the experience admit to it, but demonstrate that you are a fast learner and can learn the job. And that you believe your strengths outweigh this weakness.

Prepare Your Own Case

If you simply walk into the interview and answer each question as it's asked, without having done any preparation, you'll probably put on a fairly decent show. But if you really want this job, that's not enough. You have no idea how tough the competition is. If it's fairly weak, an unprepared interview might still get you the job. But what if it's strong? A missed opportunity – something you might have said but forgotten to mention – might tip the balance against you.

Make sure this doesn't happen. Before you get to the interview, you should already have a mental list of all of the most important points you want to make – all the things that will impress on your interviewer that you are the best person for the job.

You've already assessed yourself to establish your key strengths. Drive this home. If your strengths can be objectively measured – qualifications, skill at using particular equipment, – simply telling the interviewer that you possess them will be sufficient. But some strength – such as experience or diplomacy skills, for example – will need to be illustrated with examples.

You may be able to think of an example to illustrate your strengths on the spot when you're asked. But if you prepare in advance you won't just come up with any example, you'll come up with the best and most relevant one to the job you are applying for!

So that's your basic list of strengths. And you also need to go through the job description in much the same way, finding examples to demonstrate that you have experience in all the key areas of responsibility. If you don't have a copy of the job description (which would normally be sent out with the application form) call the interviewers office and ask them to send you one. It's standard practice so they won't mind being asked.

Your interviewer might be interested to see some evidence to back up any strength and experience that you may have. While they are unlikely to expect to see anything other than perhaps proof of qualifications, they may well be impressed by anything else you can offer them such as:

- Testimonials from satisfied customers or suppliers.
- Copies of key reports you have written.
- Examples of past work.
- Press cuttings you have generated.
- Press articles about events you have organized.
- And so on.

So, find anything you can that will help persuade them that you really are as good as look, and take it along. Clearly, it's not a good idea to turn up at the interview pushing a wheelbarrow of stuff in front of you. Take what's portable, and will fit into a neat folder – or a portfolio if it involves a lot of design or artwork. Then let the interviewer know what else you could send them – or bring to a second interview – if they want to see it.

Be Prepared for the Interview

You now know what you want to say and get certain points across. But how long have you got to say them? Have you got to cram your key selling points into 15 minutes, or have you got an hour to bring them out slowly, one by one?

The only way to find this out is by asking. Contact your interviewer's office (preferably at same time as any other requests you have to make) and simply ask, "Please could you tell me how much time has been allocated to my interview"? Again, it's a totally reasonable question and one they should be happy to answer.

You now have all the advance information you need, and all your preparation is in place. The final step is to be ready for the interview on the day itself. And you must start by being on time. It doesn't matter how early you arrive – you can always find the building and then go for a walk, for lunch or for a browse in the local shops so you don't arrive at reception too soon. But being as little as one or two minutes late may matter a lot – especially if your interviewer turns out to be a stickler for good time keeping.

Of course, you can imagine scenarios where no amount of forward planning could have got you to the interview on time. But unless the reason is highly dramatic, your interviewer doesn't want to hear excuses. They just want you to be there on time. So, do yourself a few favors:

- Leave plenty of time to get there.

- Take with you the letter inviting you for the interview, with the time on it, and any directions that have been sent.
- Enquire about parking if you're traveling by car and think it could be a problem.
- Take a mobile phone, or money for phone calls, in case you need to call for directions. Then if you do still run late, despite all your precautions, at least you can call ahead and let them know what's happening.

As well as making sure you arrive on time, you will also need to take with you:

- Your portfolio material and the directions. Mobile phone and anything else – all neatly in one briefcase or handbag.

A notepad and pen (also in the briefcase) for jotting down notes during the interview.

Your interviewers will form a large part of their opinion of you on the basis of a very small amount of the time they spend with you. In fact, the first few moments will tell them a great deal about you, whether they like you or not. Your best defense against this, of course, is to make sure you send out the right messages.

From the way you dress to the way you say hello, you can prepare yourself to give the best possible first impression. In fact, why not start before you even get to the day of the interview? You can influence your interviewer's opinion:

- Before the interview
- In the way you dress
- By the way you greet them

From various surveys of employers, they cited some of the key factors that impress about a candidate:

- Strong handshake
- Being smartly and appropriately dressed.

Factors that least impressed employers:

- Lateness
- Sloppy appearance
- Poor grooming
- Too much perfume or aftershave.

Before the Interview

Yes, even before you get to the interview, you can already generate a strong first impression. Your original application was clearly good enough to win you an interview. If it included a well presented and professional looking RESUME and application form, your interviewer will already expect a strong candidate to walk through the door. You can enhance this impression even further with:

- A well-written cover letter when you sent in your application, briefly outlining your strengths (in relation to the job in question).
- A further letter, again well-written and professionally laid out, confirming the arrangements for this interview and saying how much you are looking forward to it.

If it's too late for these now, you can still give a great first impression. But next time you apply for a job, bear these points in mind so you can make a strong, positive impression even before the interview.

Interview Attire

The way you dress for your interview will tell the employer about your professional savviness and, in some cases, will be one of the determining factors in your evaluation. Your ability to "dress the part" speaks to your knowledge of the industry and interest in "fitting in". Also, by dressing professionally, you will appear more mature and seasoned; this will aid you as you may compete with older individuals with more experience. Understand that you will probably dress more professionally for an interview than may be required once you begin to work in that environment. Appropriate interview attire will vary by field; however, you are best advised to dress professionally using the following guidelines from UCLA's 1999 Business Attire Survey:

Men and Women

- Two-piece business suit (navy or other dark color)
- Consistent look: avoid wearing a business suit with sandals or sneakers
- Well-groomed hair: avoid unusual styles or colors
- Minimal cologne or perfume
- No visible body art: cover tattoos with clothing if possible
- Breath mints; use one before greeting the recruiter
- No visible body piercings (other than earrings for women)

Women

- White, off-white, or neutral-colored blouse with a conservative neckline
- Suit with a skirt preferable to a pantsuit
- No ill-fitting skirts (short, tight, clingy, or slit)
- Closed-toe leather pumps with low to medium heels. Avoid open-toe strappy high heels, sandals, or shoes with decorations.
- Skin-colored hosiery
- Briefcase or portfolio in place of a handbag or purse
- Conservative nail polish, avoid unusual colors, e.g., blue or green
- Understated makeup
- Small stud earrings instead of dangling or oversized earrings
- Long hair pulled back in a neat, simple style. No "big hair" or elaborate styles

Men

- Long-sleeved oxford cloth shirt in white or light blue
- Conservative necktie in terms of color and pattern. Avoid cartoon characters, less-than-serious graphics, or theme ties
- High-fitting dark socks. Avoid light colored socks with a dark suit

- Business-style leather shoes
- Matching shoe and belt color. Do not mix black and brown.
- Briefcase or portfolio, no backpack

What Are You Going to Wear?

Knowing how to dress for an interview isn't what it used to be. You used to put on your best suit and tie, or your smartest tailored dress or skirt suit, and you knew you looked business. Unfortunately, things aren't so simple any more. A smart formal outfit just won't look right in an organization where the workforces all wear jeans and T – shirts. The interviewer will think "Very smart. They will never fit in here!"

So, you need to know what the dress code is at the organization you are applying. That way you can pick an appropriate outfit. You may well have a good idea of what the dress code is likely to be; it is often fairly consistent across whole industries. Design and media companies tend to dress casually; insurance brokers are likely to dress smarter. If you are changing jobs within your own industry, the odds are you will be pretty clear about the usual style.

But what if this is an industry, you're not so sure about? There are several options;

- If you know someone who works for the organization – or simply knows them as a supplier or a customer perhaps – you can ask their advice.
- If the organization is based nearby, turn up at lunchtime or going home time and watch people leaving the building to see what they are all wearing.
- Look through sales brochures and annual reports for photos of management and staff.

But failing all that, the answer is the same as usual: ask. When you're calling your contact – the interviewer, their assistant or their secretary – ask them what the company dress code is. As always, they will be happy to help and they will be impressed by your initiative.

What to wear, then? Just because you have found what the regular employees are wearing doesn't mean you are going to wear the same things yourself. After all, you're not a regular employee yet, you are attending an interview and you need to look as if you are making an extra effort. Dress a notch or two above the employees who look like they would if they were making an effort.

It's OK to remove your jacket, for example, or it isn't. But the fundamental point is the same: dress a notch or two above the people you will pass in the corridor when you go to the interview, unless they're already formally dressed, in which case you need only match them (rather than turning up in full evening dress!)

When it comes to the specifics of the outfit you choose to wear, here are a few more pointers you may find useful:

- Don't let your appearance overpower your personality. You can wear bright clothes but don't wear something so unusual it steals all the attention. It's you applying for the job not your clothes!
- Avoid any extremes of fashion.
- Avoid strong perfume or aftershave.
- Don't wear too much jewelry, or jewelry that is too large.

- Avoid large patterns in bright colors, unless restricted to a small area such as a tie or scarf.
- Dark colors will lend you more authority than pale ones.

When you arrive for the interview (don't forget to be on time!) ask the receptionist to direct you somewhere where you can freshen up. Tidy your hair and check your clothes, and double check your;

- Teeth (especially if you have just eaten).
- Nose.
- Jewelry (especially earrings for women).
- Zips and buttons (especially flies for men).
- Shirt or blouse (make sure they're tucked in).
- Make up.

It is worthwhile, if you're a woman, to take a spare pair of tights (if you're wearing tights). Likewise, if you're a man, it's worth bringing along a spare tie just in case you spill food
or drink down the first one. Alternatively, don't put your tie on until you reach the building.

Your Opening Greeting

As well as the way you look, the way you greet the interviewer will also be an important part of the first impression you create. **So be ready to exude warmth and confidence** as soon as you see them. The key points to remember are:

- Smile.
- Make eye contact with the interviewer.
- Offer a hand to shake as soon as they introduce themselves.
- Say "Hello", "Pleased to meet you", or whatever phrase you feel comfortable with.
- Shake hands firmly (you can practice your handshake with a friend) – with all interviewers if there is more than one.
- Wait to be invited before you sit down.

The interviewer will generally talk for a few minutes in the beginning to put you at your ease. Be responsive, but remember that neither of you is here to chat. When they ask, for example, how your journey was, they don't want a blow-by-blow account of it. A friendly but brief response will be fine. And if by chance it was horrendous, express the fact (if you mention it at all) with humor rather than sounding like a winger.

Almost all of us feel nervous before an important interview. After all, it's something that matters to us that we need to get right. Nerves are only natural.

Interview Tips

- Shake hands firmly.
- Look the employer in the eye when you are talking.
- Speak clearly, don't mumble.
- If you need time to think before you answer, take the time. Stick to the subject at hand, which is the job and your skills related to it.

- Use the employer's name, pronounce it correctly.
- Don't fidget in your seat and otherwise show nervousness with your body (hands, posture, etc.).
- Don't take notes during the interview if you can help it.
- Don't complain about a former boss or co-worker. By complaining, you are likely to make the employer think that you are hard to get along with.
- Don't ask about salaries, sick leaves, pensions, vacations, or benefits on the first interview.
- Don't exaggerate; state the facts.
- If you have specific qualifications for a job, be sure to let the employer know about them. No one knows what you can do unless you tell them.
- Talk about school subjects and hobbies that you have done well in and which are related to the job for which you are applying.
- An employer may be interested in everything you can do, **but will be most interested in your skills that relate to the job for which you are applying.**
- **Ask questions when you don't understand what the employer is talking about**. You'll want to know as much about the job as you can and asking questions is the best way to find out.
- The interviewers will close when they have enough information - don't try to extend the interview unless you have an important point to make which has not been covered-then cover it, but make it brief.
- Before you leave the interview (assuming you want the position), let the employer know that you really want the job. By doing this, the employer will feel that you will work hard and that you will want to stay on the job.

Internal Applicants

If you are applying for a job within your own organization can you expect the interview to follow the same format? The answer is yes. The interviewer can only assess all the candidates equally if they have interviewed them all on an equal basis. That means everyone should be allocated the same amount of time, given the same amount of respect and privacy and asked the same questions whether they are external or internal applicants.

Just because your interviewer may know the answer to some of the questions already, for example "How well do you work under pressure?" they still want to hear your answer to the question. Don't say, "That's a stupid question, you already know how I work under pressure" just give them the answer you would if this was an external interview.

You can expect the interview to follow the same format if you are an internal applicant whom they already know, as they would if you were applying from outside the organization. However, you don't have to pretend you've never met before! They will lead the opening few minutes by chatting informally and they are likely to behave as they normally do rather than pretend you are a stranger; this will help to set the tone.

Don't make a big thing of your internal status, cracking in jokes or being personal – even in a positive way – about colleagues. But there is no need to pretend that the interviewer doesn't know what you're talking about when they do. You may find it easier to answer questions as you would to an outside interviewer but add phrases such as "You will remember…." or "As you well know…."

Be Strong and Courageous

The key lies in understanding what causes a nerves attack. And the root is fear. Fear of what could go wrong, from drying up completely to soaking the interviewer by spilling your coffee. The more remote these failures and catastrophes seem, the more remote your fears will be. This is why you often notice a couple of minutes into an interview you're not nearly as nervous as you were just before you began: things are going fine, you realize you're not making a complete fool of yourself and you seem to be able to hold a normal conversation after all.

If you can minimize the likelihood of things going wrong, you will minimize your fear. There will still be a small irrational panic at the very back of your mind, at least until the interview is under way, but it need cause no more than a touch of adrenaline which simply keeps you thinking fast.

Your best bet is to rehearse as thoroughly as you can. Think through your answers to likely questions and tough ones and practice your answers in front of a mirror. Rehearse your opening greeting. Try your outfit on in advance if you haven't worn it recently.

But you will still want to take other precautions. Your motto should be: be prepared. Anticipate disaster, consider every possible emergency or embarrassment you can, and plan for it. That way, it won't happen or –even if it does – you'll be ready to cope. Here are some antidotes to one or two classic adrenaline – starters:

Coffee and Tea – If you're worried, you'll spill them, simply decline them when offered. In fact, caffeine is not a great idea anyway if you are nervous – avoid it for a couple of hours prior to your interview (along with any form of alcohol).

Looking Nervous – Actually, no one cares if you look nervous as long as you do the job well. But we often fear to appear nervous. If you are inclined to shake at the start of the interview, fold your hands together in your lap where they can keep each other under control.

Mouth Turning Dry – When you turn down the coffee, ask for a glass of water instead. If you don't need it, it's OK to leave it (you don't have to drink it and have the worry of spilling it).

Unable to think of – Here's another time the glass of water comes in handy. Taking a sip

Anything to Say – Or two before you answer a question buys you a few moments to get your head straight.

Fumbling with Briefcase –Take into the interview just a single envelope file. Leave the rest of

Spilling Papers – Check your stuff in at reception.

Difficult Questions – Get someone to role-play a question and answer session with you and brief them to be as difficult as possible. That way, the real thing will be a breeze by comparison.

Easing the Symptoms

As far as coping with the physical symptoms of nervousness; try to eat before the interview. Don't binge, but a light breakfast or lunch will help (unless you honestly think you'll bring it straight back up). Nerves are always worse on an empty stomach.

You may also find relaxation exercises helpful. The way to reduce stress is to relax and slow breathing is a quick fix for this. Here's an exercise, which you can do moments before your interview, for example while you're waiting at reception:

- Sit down if possible, but you can do this standing up if necessary.
- Relax your arms and hands. If you're sitting down, put your hands in your lap.
- Close your eyes if you can but this isn't essential.
- Breathe in through your nose, slowly, to a count of five. Breathe in as low down as you can, pushing out your diaphragm and stomach.
- Breathe out through your mouth to a count of seven. If you are sitting down, don't slump as you breathe out.
- Allow your breathing to return to normal and open your eyes.

You can repeat this at intervals as often as you need to, but always let your breathing return to normal in between. If you don't, you may hyperventilate. This won't do you any harm, but it can make you feel a little light headed which may make you more nervous rather than more relaxed.

Even when the interview is under way, there are techniques you can use on the spot to help you relax:

- Take a deep breath while the interviewer is asking you a question. The more tense we get, the more our ribs and chest lock up. By releasing them with a deep, chest expanding breath, you ease the tension so it can't build up. This requires no concentration, so you can still focus on what the interviewer is asking you.
- Smiling helps relax your muscles. You may feel like an idiot if you grin inanely throughout the interview, but if you can find opportunities to smile as you begin to respond to a question it will relax you. And it will help you come across as a warm and friendly person, too.
- If you notice yourself sitting hunched up, legs and arms crossed (not to mention fingers and toes!!), shift to a more open and relaxed position. The important thing for relaxation is just to open up and allow your muscles to relax.

Your muscles may tense up as a result of psychological nervousness, but you can reverse the cause and effect: relaxing your muscles can make you feel at ease.

The Interview Process

The Format

Virtually every interview follows the same basic format. The interview generally consists of five interrelated stages: introduction and icebreaker; verifying information and asking questions; responding to your questions; closing the interview and decision-making.

1. After an initial brief conversation, the interviewer will ask you questions from a general list that all candidates will be asked from.

2. Next, they will ask you specific questions from your own application or resume. These will be questions such as "I see that you have been with your current employer 12 months. Why are you looking to move so soon?"

3. The interviewer will probably tell you a little bit more about the organization and what the job entails. After this they may come back to earlier points and probe further if they are still unsure.

4. A seasoned interviewer will explain the decision-making process and provide information concerning future steps. If the interviewer does not specifically give this information, it is appropriate for you to ask about follow-up procedures. Be sure to ask the interviewer for their business card; this information will be helpful as you prepare your thank you letter.

The first interview you will encounter is called a screening interview. It may take place on campus (through the On-campus Interview Program), at a job fair, or at the employer's office. This type of interview generally lasts 30 minutes to one hour. The purpose of the screening interview is to separate unqualified applicants from qualified ones. An invitation for a second interview may be offered in a few days from the screening interview or it may take up to four weeks. Usually, only a small percentage of candidates will be invited back for the second interview.

The second interview is an in-depth interview conducted at the site of the organization. It may last anywhere from one hour to two days. Some employers may even call you back three or four times before making a decision regarding your candidacy.

Having carefully prepared for this moment, you should approach the interview with confidence. Each interview will be different; some interviews will be very structured and formal while others may be casual and informal. Interviewing styles will vary.

After the interview, the employer will assess your qualifications and determine "fit" between you and the position. This is also a time for you to evaluate your interest in the position. Immediately following your interview, take time to write down questions you were asked, general impressions, and questions that you may now have as result of the interview. Also, evaluate your interviewing skills and consider ways you can improve for your next interview. Remember to send a thank you letter to the employer within 24 hours after your interview.

The Second Interview

Very few employment offers are made after a screening interview. Before an offer is extended, an employer will generally require a second interview. Being invited for a second interview indicates that the employer has sincere interest in you as a candidate; however, it does not mean that a job offer is pending. Again, it is your responsibility to prepare for the interview and do your best to market your skills and abilities. Before accepting the invitation, carefully assess your interest in the organization. Only accept an invitation for a second interview if you have an interest in the organization.

A second interview may last from one hour to two full days; the most typical interviews last from four to six hours. If the interview is within driving distance, be sure to confirm directions and parking instructions. You may even want to drive to the location a day or two in advance to alleviate any logistical concerns; you don't want to get lost on your way to the interview and arrive late.

If your second interview requires long distance travel, a company representative will generally make airline and hotel arrangements for you. Be sure to ask this representative if other expenses, such as meals, will be prepaid or if you should plan on paying for these expenses and submitting receipts.

Before your interview, you should receive a schedule which includes the names and titles of the people with whom you will meet. If you do not receive a schedule, you should call and ask for this information. Be sure to know the name of the person for whom you should ask when you arrive on site. Plan to arrive 15 minutes early so you can check your appearance and collect your thoughts prior to the start of your interviews. As always, politely greet the receptionist or others you may meet while waiting on your interview.

Throughout the course of the day, you may meet with a number of employees. Pay close attention to their names and titles. A title may help you understand the type of response that particular individual is seeking. For example, if the interviewer is a manager, they may look at work ethic as well as general knowledge; if the interviewer is a potential colleague, they may look for someone who is a team player; if the interviewer is the financial manager of the organization, their questions will probably center on your knowledge and experience in budgeting and finance.

You should prepare for the second interview just as you did for the screening interview: thoroughly review your research on the organization, gathering additional information if possible, and be prepared to demonstrate a match between your qualifications and the position. Excellent communication skills are very important at this stage.

Responding Positively

Follow these guidelines when you answer questions. All of these are aimed at giving the interviewer a positive view of you as someone who is confident, capable and honest.

- Don't ramble. Aim for all your answers to be no more than two minutes at the most, but many should of course be shorter. At the other end of the spectrum as

previously mentioned try and avoid one-word answers unless you are being asked to clarify something.
- Use Examples. Give plenty of specific examples of your achievements, challenges and successes. Be prepared to back up every assertion and demonstrate every skill or achievement with a concrete example.
- Remember the job description. Keep your answers specific to the job in question. For example, if your interviewer asks you what your greatest strength is pick one which will be important to this job – and give an example of it.
- Pause If You Need To. If you need to think for a moment before answering a question that is fine. It shows that you are considering your answer carefully.
- DON'T LIE. Be as honest as you can in your answers. You can – and should – put a positive spin on the truth, but don't change the facts. This includes admitting if you don't know the answer to a question rather than floundering and looking flustered.
- Don't Criticize Your Current Employer. If you are new to the job market, don't degenerate your tutor or your college course. It can make you look negative and picky (and the interviewer may wonder what the other side of the story is), and it will certainly make your interviewer question your loyalty.

Many experts consider the following as key do's and don'ts when handling interviews:

Do:

- Answer the question asked and do not volunteer irrelevant information.
- Keep your answers concise and concentrate on the facts not opinions.
- Speak clearly and confidently and do not allow yourself to be discouraged.
- Constantly remind yourself that you have something to sell and focus on how you can make a positive contribution in the role.

Don't:

- Try to be too clever – no one likes a "holier than thou".
- Lie, pretend or give evasive answers.
- Lose your temper, get flustered or panic.
- Criticize your current or previous employers.

Making an Exit

The interviewer will signal when the interview is over. And just like any good sales person you may not expect to clinch a deal on the spot but you will at least want to agree on the next step. So, ask what happens next and when. You want to know whether there will be a second round of interviews, whether you'll hear by phone or by letter, when they'll be in touch and so on.

Apart from that when the interview ends, stand up, collect your things and leave promptly. Before you leave shake the interviewer's hand if they offer you a hand. Thank them for seeing you and smile warmly (however you feel inside) and make a clean exit.

If the interviewer walks you to reception or to the main exit talking as you go remember that you are still on show. Don't be fooled by the official end of the interview into making any unguarded comments.

There are some questions that you can expect to be asked at most interviews so these are the ones you should really be prepared for. There are certain things an interviewer is bound to want to know about you, and these are reflected in these questions. They will often come in the first half of the interview, since these typically are questions that the interviewer will ask all the candidates.

We will list some of the general questions but first we will look at some general guidelines, which apply to every answer you, give. The key things to remember when you answer any question are:

- *Keep Your Answer Relevant* – if you are asked to outline your strengths don't give a long list. Pick one or two key areas. You may have a dozen strengths but just pick the ones your interviewer most needs the successful applicant for this job to have.
- *Listen to the Question and Answer the Question You've Been Asked* – don't sidestep difficult questions. Your interviewer isn't stupid – they'll notice what you are doing it and won't like it.
- *Answer Only the Question You Are Asked* – don't give lots of superfluous information. Keep your answers as brief as you can without omitting anything relevant.

Saying *Thank You*

Write a thank you note before the interviewers have time to make their decision. The letter doesn't have to be written on paper you could e-mail your interviewer to make sure that they get it as soon as possible. Your letter has four basic functions:

- It gives you a chance to remind the interviewer of who you are.
- It shows that you have good manners and are courteous.
- It gives you a chance to mention anything important that you missed saying during the interview.
- It shows that you really are committed to get the job.

Very few people bother write a thank you letter after an interview, so it will certainly bring attention to your name on the list. Moreover, it may bring your name to the forefront of the interviewer's mind and it may also help you if you had slipped down the list a little. It can make the difference between getting on the shortlist for the final interview.

What does the letter need to say? Only you can decide what to put in your letter but it could be something along the lines of "Thank you for giving me the opportunity to meet with you this afternoon. I very much enjoyed the interview and would confirm that I am still very interested in the job. Should there be anything further you would like me to clarify please contact me on my mobile number provided on the top of my RESUME. I look forward to hear from you in due time." It might be that there was something you forgot to tell them about yourself at the interview and you could add this but keep it brief and only add it if it really is relevant. The idea is for the interviewer to read and remember the letter not having to spend fifteen minutes reading it.

Waiting

The interview was wonderful (you thought) and the interviewer said she would get in touch with you (but that was four weeks ago) and you are going crazy! Waiting can cause stress and anguish. You need to remember that no one makes you wait for nothing. Before you panic, try to recall if the interviewer indicated the time frame for selection. It may be weeks or a month before an employer is able to get back to you regarding a decision. If you do not hear from the interviewer in the time frame discussed (always allowing a few extra days), follow up with a phone call to inquire about the status of your application.

Common reasons for a delay in response from an employer include:

- You are on a second list and the employer is still following up with the first list. Depending on the percentage of acceptances from the first list, the employer may invite you for a second interview.
- The employer is interviewing all possible sources and it is taking longer than anticipated.
- Office emergencies, that have nothing to do with you, are requiring immediate attention.

If you have any questions about the "right" thing to do or if you are feeling anxious, talk with a career counselor.

The Offer Letter

When you have agreed on everything with your employer and the contract has been finalized the company will issue you a letter formally offering you the position. This letter should outline the following areas clearly:

- The job position offered.
- The salary or remuneration.
- The starting date of employment.
- The location.
- Any conditions to which the offer is subject.
- The timescale and procedure for acceptance or rejection of the offer.

Excellent, you've received your offer letter and all the information is correct. Now, all you need to do is to respond and agree with the terms as it will be legally binding.

General Interview Questions

Below are some questions an interviewer may ask on the interview. You should be prepared to answer some of them before you walk in to the interview.

General Information
- Tell me about yourself.
- What are your interests/hobbies?
- Who has been a role model for you?

Educational Background
- Why did you attend your college?
- How did you decide on your major?
- Which class(es) did you enjoy most?
- Which class(es) did you like least?
- Based on your understanding of this position, which classes have best prepared you for this job?
- How would your professors describe you?
- What is your GPA?
- If you could change anything about your undergraduate education, what would it be?

Work History
- Tell me about your previous jobs/internships?
- Which job did you enjoy most? Why?
- What are the three most important skills you developed in your previous jobs/internships?
- How would former employers describe you?

Career Interests
- What are your career goals?
- Why are you interested in this position?
- What do you know about our company/agency?
- Why are you interested in our company/agency?
- What are your long-term career goals?
- What economic, political and/or social trends do you think will impact our industry/system in the near future?

Skills

- What experience do you have in campus or community activities?
- What have you learned/gained from your extracurricular activities?

Motivation

- What distinguishes you from other candidates?
- Is there anything else that you would like to tell me regarding your qualifications?
- Why should I hire you?

Inappropriate Questions

In most interviews, the questions you will be asked are standard and relevant to the position for which you are applying. However, in rare situations, you may be asked questions that make you feel uncomfortable or seem irrelevant to the position at hand. State and federal laws regulate the type of questions an employer can ask. Questions concerning marital status, family, or religious beliefs are considered "inappropriate" in most situations. An exception may be if you are applying for a counselor or teacher position in a religious organization.

If you feel that the questions asked are inappropriate, you have three choices when responding. First, if you are not offended and do not feel that your response will hurt your candidacy; you may answer the question directly. Second, you could refuse to answer stating that you are uncomfortable with the question; in many instances, this type of response will probably cause the employer to reject you as a candidate. However, you should consider if you would feel comfortable working for the employer in the first place. Third, you may answer the question in an indirect way. For example, if the employer asked about your marital status due to the long hours that will be required, you may respond by saying that you are fully aware of the work schedule and are willing to commit the necessary hours. Following is a partial list of illegal inappropriate interview questions:

- Are you married? Single? Divorced? Engaged? Living with anyone? Do you see your ex-spouse?
- Do you have children at home? How old? Who cares for them? Do you plan to have more children?
- How tall are you? How much do you weigh?
- Have you ever been arrested, convicted, or spent time in jail?
- If you served in any of the armed forces, what type of discharge do you have? What branch did you serve in?
- How old are you?
- Do you own your home? Do you rent? Do you live in an apartment or a house?
- Are you a U.S. citizen? (Employers may ask if you have the proper work permits or are legally able to work in the US.)
- What clubs or social organizations do you belong to?

The Art of Interviewing

Practice Makes Perfect

Interviewing is a skill. You are encouraged to anticipate interview questions and plan your responses. Start by preparing for general questions regarding education, grades, work experience and interests.

Preparing your responses can take on many forms. For some, jotting down an outline may help in preparing; for others, practicing verbal responses will be more effective. It is not enough to simply read the questions; you should plan your response.

Making a Good First Impression

As cliché as it may sound, you will not get a second chance to make a first impression when it comes to interviews. Your nonverbal skills and the manner you present yourself will be evaluated in addition to your verbal responses.

Be sure to arrive for your interview 10-15 minutes early. This will provide you with time to check your appearance and collect your thoughts prior to the interview. As you wait on the interviewer to greet you, be sure to position yourself so that you have a good view of the hall or reception area from which you expect the employer to enter.

When the employer greets you, be sure to stand and offer a firm handshake. Look the employer in the eyes and offer a return greeting similar to, "Nice to meet you." If the employer mispronounces your name, clearly state your name as you shake their hand.

The only thing that you should carry is a portfolio with paper and pen; leave your coat and belongings in the waiting area unless otherwise instructed. You are always encouraged to take an extra copy of your resume with you for all interviews. For on-site interviews, women may also carry a small, professional looking purse.

As you enter the interview room, wait for the employer to indicate where you should seat. After the employer is seated, it is your cue to also take a seat. During the interview, remember to practice good nonverbal skills:

- Sit up straight with your shoulders back and hands resting in your lap.
- Place both feet on the floor.
- Maintain eye contact to demonstrate interest and enthusiasm.
- Use limited hand gestures to emphasize key points.

Essential Qualities

Be Responsive

Make an effort to give full (but not rambling) answers to your interviewer's questions, and to volunteer relevant information. Don't give one – word answers – they sound sullen and unhelpful, even if that's not your intention. If you are asked "I see that you trained originally in sales," don't just say, "Yes" expand on your answer for example "Yes, I did. In my first sales job I specialized in advertising and I really enjoyed cold calling and found it very rewarding, hence I moved to a marketing company."

Be Confident

You may be feeling anything but confident, but confidence is an attractive quality in a candidate so you need to show you have it. Research shows that interviewers don't like to give jobs to people who put themselves down. Of course, this doesn't mean that you should be pushy and arrogant, but don't apologize for yourself. If your interviewer says "So it has been three years since you did any actual face to face selling" don't say "I'm afraid so". Say something along the lines of "Yes but it's one of those skills I feel you never lose once you have learned it."

Be Energetic

People who project life and energy come across as so much more positive, capable and even inspiring than those who seem flat and sluggish. Stay upbeat, sit up and straight, speak clearly and make eye contact (with all the interviewers if there's more than one).

Be Enthusiastic

This is closely related to being energetic and is on par with it. You can see that enthusiasm towards the job and the position is important to interviewers. The best way to transmit this enthusiasm is by seeming interested in what both you and the interviewer are saying. If you genuinely are interested, you shouldn't find this too difficult – just make sure you let it show.

Body Language

The way you come across visually can be as important as the way you come across verbally. When attending an interview, you should sit as follows:

- Don't perch on the edge of your chair. Sit well back in it – unless it's a very deep, upholstered chair in which case there's a danger of looking too relaxed if you get lost right in the back of it.
- Sit with both feet on the floor, leaning slightly towards the interviewer – inquisitively.
- Make frequent eye contact with the interviewer. If there is more than one of them, make eye contact with them all but look predominantly at whichever one asked the question you are about to answer.
- Smile.
- Don't hide your face with your hands.
- Do not send defensive signals by crossing your arms and your legs.
- Try to keep your hands still except when you're gesturing. Don't play with your hair or put your hands in your pockets.
- Wait for the interviewer to finish their question before you give your answer.

It is good to know what the optimum body language signals are but don't get hung up on them. If you are projecting the right qualities and feeling the appropriate emotions, the body language will follow naturally. But if you sense that you are flagging, that you sound less positive than you would like to, you can monitor your body language and adapt it in order to lift your mood and your verbal tone.

During an Interview - Projecting the Right Image

You must realize the importance of first impressions, it doesn't however, stop there. You have to continue to give the best possible impression throughout the interview. Quite apart from what you say, the way you say it will have a bigger impact on your interviewer's opinion of you – and whether you are the best person for the job.

But your natural personality will have many different qualities, and you need to make sure it is the positive and relevant ones, which stand out at interview. So, projecting the right image is about being you, but using the behaviors, which will most impress your interviewer.

Qualities that most influence interviewers and their order:

- Your personality and how you present yourself in the interview.
- Your experience.
- The qualifications you have for the position.
- Your background and references.
- The enthusiasm you have towards the organization and position.

All five of these qualities are important and you need to demonstrate your suitability in each area. They are in the correct order of importance. Yes, how you come across in an interview is the single most important factor that will determine if you get the job or not. What do you need to do?

Market Your Skills

After you have analyzed the position and researched the organization, you are now in a position to review your qualifications for the position. Knowing what you have to offer is crucial. Expressing yourself clearly and concisely is a key element of effective interviewing. Self-assessment of your skills, interests, and work values will help you organize your thoughts in order to project a positive impression. A thorough self-assessment should enable you to:

- Summarize your educational experiences as it relates to the position for which you are interviewing.
- Articulate your related skills and abilities.
- Cite examples of how you developed/used particular skills.
- Know your personal strengths and weaknesses.
- Discuss your work and co-curricular experiences in detail.
- Talk about your career goals and objectives.
- Know where you want to work.
- Identify any problem areas in your background and be prepared to discuss them.
- Discuss variables you are willing to negotiate (e.g. salary for geographical preference.

Tell me about yourself.

This is not an invitation to give your life history. In fact, you really need to ask the interviewer to be more specific before you can answer. Ask them "What aspect of myself would you like me to tell you about?" They are most likely to ask you to talk about what you are like at work.

You should aim to describe yourself in a couple of minutes at the most. Concentrate on positive qualities and link them to the key responsibilities of the job to which you are applying. Should they ask to hear about what you are like away from work you will still want to give them an answer which means you are cut out for the job. We are not suggesting that you lie. You've got plenty of time to think about this question before you get to the interview and be ready with suitable and honest answers about your personal or business life.

Sell me this pen.

This is an interesting question and some employers will ask you to do this even if you aren't applying for a sales job. The reason behind this is to see if you focus on the benefits of the object rather than its features. This is all about the bigger picture. If you outline the benefits it will impress them! Of course, it doesn't have to be a pen it can be a notebook, paperweight or anything else on the interviewer's desk.

Tell me a story.

This question is tricky. The idea is to see if you are sharp enough to ask for the question to be more specific before you answer. The sound response will be to ask the interviewer "What type of story do you want me to tell?" Usually they ask for a story about you and will more than likely specify whether they want a work related or personal story. It's then up to you to come up with a tale that shows you in a good light.

What do you think the role of a (whatever the job is)?

You should have thought this question through before. We can't tell you the answer since we don't know what your job is but you need to answer the following:

- The overall objective of the job
- The key responsibilities of the job.

As you may realize, you can pick up clues from the job description if you are applying for a job in your usual line of work. But you will also want to draw on your own experience.

What do you know about our company?

This is a great opportunity for you to show that you have done your homework. State the relevant points – size, turnover, nature of the business, growth and business ethos (for example, "I know you are a young, growing organization with a reputation for developing people"). Keep it brief, but add one or two things that suggest you've gone deeper than merely reading the annual report. For example, "I notice in the trade press that you've just signed a couple of very large deals with Weston & Weston."

Why do you want this job?

Try not to waffle on about challenges and prospects. Talk in terms of benefits for them and be specific about the kind of challenge you enjoy. For example, "I am a great organizer and I'm looking for a position that gives me scope to plan and organize." This is also a great opportunity to show off the research you've done into the company – again keeping it brief and relevant.

Why do you want to leave your present job?

It doesn't matter if the real reason is that you can't stand working with your boss any longer, or that the company pays terrible wages. Keep that to yourself. The interviewer is looking for a positive reason for moving forward, not a negative aim to avoid a job you are not happy in. The only good answer to this question is "Because I want to broaden my experience and I think I can do that better in a new organization" (or something along those lines).

What do you feel you can bring to this job?

This is another question that gives you a chance to shine. You need to link your past experiences or skills to the requirements of the job. So, pick three or four key strong points in your favor, which are relevant to this job.

What are your greatest strengths?

This is a perfect question – just focus your answers on the key responsibilities of the job to make sure your strengths are relevant to your interviewer. And make sure you don't waffle on for too long; pick one or two key strengths, which are very important for this job.

What is your biggest weakness?

This is a hard one. You don't want to sound negative. Use one of the following as your defense:

- Humor ("I have a sweet tooth!").
- Something personal, which isn't work related (I like watching soccer on Sundays).
- Something that was relevant years ago (when I first started in my career, I was hopeless with paperwork but I am now disciplined and sort all of my paperwork.
- Something that your interviewer will see as a strength (Once I get started with something, I just can't put it down until I've finished.)

All of these answers should avoid giving away any true weaknesses and they also avoid making you come across as arrogant or too perfect – something that really irritates an interviewer.

Where do you see yourself in five years?

You need to be careful how you answer this because if you give a specific goal and the interviewer knows that they cannot fulfill it, they will put off employing you. But remember that they want to know that you are driven and will keep increasing your value to them.

How long do you expect to stay with this company?

The interviewer isn't going to employ someone who is going to be off again before they've got their full value from them. Indicate that you'd like to stay a few years. "I'd like to settle with this company and grow and develop within it. I see myself staying as long as I keep progressing here and making a valuable contribution."

What motivates you?

You need to give an answer, as always, that benefits your potential employer and links into the key responsibilities of the job. Don't say "$ 100,000 a year and a Bentley Continental!" Give an answer along the lines of "I'm happiest when I can see a project through from start to finish."

How do you approach a typical project?

If you are applying for a project-based job, such as project manager, you will definitely be asked this question. You don't need to give a long-winded answer but you should demonstrate that you would take into account the main components of effective project planning such as:

- Plan the schedule backwards from completion/delivery date.
- Work out what you need to get the job done effectively and on time.
- Budget cost, time and resources.
- Allow for contingencies.

How well do you take direction?

Keep in mind that your interviewer may become your boss should you get the job, so remember that you will take their directions. Say that you take direction well. You can add credibility to your answer by expanding and adding something like "I don't see how a team can function effectively unless its members are happy to take directions from their leader".

How do you handle criticism?

Remember your interviewer may anticipate becoming your boss and will inevitably have to criticize you from time to time. They want to know if this task will be easy for them or if you will make their lives difficult.

You could answer this question along the lines of "I'm always happy to be given constructive criticism and welcome this. It helps me learn from my mistakes and improve my performance".

Describe a situation in which your work was criticized.

Interviewers may ask you this question – or a variation of it – if they want to see how you cope with tough questioning. So, make sure you have an answer ready just in case. You should answer in a couple of stages:

- Briefly describe the task and the criticism you received for it.
- Explain how you learn from it and you haven't repeated such mistakes since.

Not only does this make you look human (which we all are including interviewers) and as though you haven't been criticized for a long time, but it also shows that you can take constructive criticism and learn from it.

Do you enjoy doing routine tasks?

It's unlikely that you will be asked this question unless the job entails carrying out routine tasks, however bearing in mind that most jobs have an element of "tedious" work then this may come up. Your answer could be "Yes, I get satisfaction from all aspects of my job and enjoy carrying out all of my duties successfully".

How do you operate under stress?

Again, this is a question you will be asked only if it is relevant to the job. A good full answer will serve you better on this one rather than a brief one. Tell your interviewer that you work well under pressure and if you really do enjoy it tell them. It's always good to give an example of a situation that you have handled where there has been a large amount of pressure. It might be prudent to add that you operate good time management and organizational skills, which help you, deal with pressurized situations and minimize stress levels.

What do you dislike most at work?

"NOTHING!" The interviewer can hire you safely knowing that you will be well motivated every minute of the working day and every moment of your working time with your employer. So, if they ask you this question your answer will be "you can't think of anything you dislike about work."

What were your most significant achievements in your current job?

It's unlikely that this job will require exactly the same achievements as the last – although it's great if you can find a clear parallel. What the interviewer really wants to know is the qualities you must have exhibited in order to receive the accolade. Be ready with something, which is:

- Recent (or the implication is you've achieved little of note since)
- Difficult to achieve
- As relevant as possible to the job you are applying for.

If you could start again, what career decisions would you make differently?

You are on a hiding to nothing if you start trying to think of hypothetical improvements to your past career. Anything you say will suggest that you are not happy with the way things are – and why would anyone want to hire someone who doesn't really want to be where they are?

The only reasonable answer is that you wouldn't change anything; you are happy with things as they are now. You might add something like "I'm not the kind of person to look back with regrets. I like to invest my energy in looking forward".

Do you consider that your career so far has been a success?

It's clearly better to be a success than a failure. To expand on this answer (as you always should on a one-word answer), you can go on to define success in your own terms. This is particularly sensible if your career on paper may look less than outstanding, even if it's respectable.

There's no point in pretending your resume glitters when it clearly doesn't – so show you are positive and looking ahead: "I've had one or two career problems in the past, but those are firmly behind me. From now on I intend to build on the good breaks I've had and enjoy a very successful career".

How does this job fit into your career plan?

It's fairly unwise to commit yourself too precisely to a career plan. So, you might say something like "Business changes so rapidly nowadays it's hard to plan precisely. But I know what I want to get ahead in this industry and I think the opportunities to do that in this company are excellent".

What appeals to you least about this job?

You need to be careful with this one. Naming almost anything will give the interviewer the impression that you are less than 100% enthusiastic about this job. Either tell them what appeals to you, or if you don't feel happy with this kind of answer come up with a part of the job which is:

- A small part of it.
- Of no major importance.
- Universally unpopular.

How long would it take you to make a useful contribution to this company?

You might think that you can't answer this question without more information and you'd be right. So, ask for more information:

- What would my key objectives be for the first six months?
- Are there any specific projects you would need me to start working on straight away?

You can use the answers to these enquiries to help you with your answer. But broadly speaking you should indicate that (unless there is an urgent project) you would expect to spend the first week or two settling in and finding your way around. After that you'd expect to make a useful contribution within the first few weeks and to show significant successes within four to six months.

Describe a situation which, in hindsight, you could have handled better.

The trick here is to be ready with something from a long time ago. Try to prepare an example where it really wasn't your fault you handled it as you did. For example, "I was well prepared for a presentation, but the facility had last-minute technical issues, so hindsight, I make sure to always have printed copies of my presentation on hand."

What sort of decisions do you find difficult to make?

You've never found a decision difficult to make in your life of course. But the danger with some of these questions is that if you could come across as arrogant. You have to admit to some minor failings but make sure they have been overcome or are irrelevant to the job you are applying for – otherwise make them sound human – no one is perfect. You could say something like "The kind of decisions I dislike most are the ones which others won't like. They aren't actually difficult but for example I don't like having to make the decision to sack someone".

What sort of people do you find difficult to work with?

You don't want to criticize others. Don't tell them about Phil in personnel who is absolutely useless at getting your expenses check back on time – it doesn't carry any weight. Start by saying that you are an easy going person who gets along with people easily because of your nature, but if you had to pick a type of person that niggles you it will be the one who doesn't pull his weight or isn't bothered about the standard of their work because it reflects badly on the rest of the team.

What do you enjoy most in your current job?

This question can be tricky. The interviewer is tempting you to indicate that there are things you don't like about your job. If that's so, presumably there will be things about this job that you don't like too – which isn't very encouraging. So, the only answer you can really give is to say that you enjoy everything about your job.

If you think this sounds a little implausible you can pick out one or two especial favorite parts of the job – making sure that they will be important parts of this job too, should you get it. You might say "I'm blessed really. I can't think of anything I don't enjoy about my job. But I suppose the thing I enjoy the most is dealing directly with customers. That's why I've applied for this job; because I'd like the opportunity to spend even more of my time doing it."

What is the biggest challenge you've faced at work?

As long as you are prepared, this is a great question. You need to have an answer ready for it. The idea is to describe the challenge, but also to show how you coped with it. You need to pick an example, which leaves you looking good.

There is something else behind this question: the interviewer is also finding what you consider to be a challenge. So, think hard about the example you want to pick. Will it be a tough decision? A difficult situation? A system that needed overhauling to improve results? You get to choose, so pick something that's relevant to this job.

How would your colleagues describe you?

This is an invitation to list your strong points. Concentrate on your plus points as a colleague – supportive, a good team player etc. As with all these questions, it's unwise to make any outrageous claims.

How would your friends describe you?

"What friends?" is not the right answer. In fact, it runs along much the same lines, as "How would your colleagues describe you?" Don't be unrealistic about yourself, but pick your strong points, which will be relevant. It's always worth mentioning **loyalty and supportiveness.**

The interviewer is simply trying to get a more rounded picture of the kind of person you are, to help them assess whether you'll fit in with the people you'll be working with.

What would your boss say about you?

Your interviewer may be your future boss so you need to answer this question carefully. They want to know that you are an effective worker, but they don't want you to step on their toes. Describe yourself, as any boss would want to see you. For example, "My boss would describe me as a hard-working, conscientious, loyal and easy to motivate employee. He'd say that I work exceptionally well on my own initiative and I'm a supportive member of the team."

What outside interests do you have?

Your interviewer is trying to know you better. Your interests will tell them whether you are sporty, competitive, enjoy dangerous pursuits or like solo or group activities and so on. Don't invent hobbies that you don't do, but select those hobbies or interests, which show you as the kind of person your interviewer is looking for.

What have you read and enjoyed lately?

Don't make up some fashionable answer here, or name a leading business book you haven't actually read. You may be asked questions about your answer. You don't have to mention the most recent book you've read so pick one you genuinely enjoyed which is slightly offbeat – which may make you stand out from the rest.

We know all interview questions are tough but these are the real hard ones! Generally, these questions aren't asked to make your life difficult or to make you squirm they are simply asked so that the interviewer can find out what he wants to know in the best possible way. As far as the interviewer is concerned this isn't a competition, you are both on the same side so there is no point in trying to get the better of you or knock you down a peg or two. Tough questions are only tough because you aren't sure how to answer them.

Whether or not the interviewer's questions are intended to be tough you should always follow these rules:

- Stay calm.
- Don't get defensive.
- Pause for a short moment before you answer if you feel better doing this.

What is your present boss like?

Never criticize any of your bosses – current, former or otherwise. The interviewer may be your future boss and wants to see you being loyal to other bosses even behind their backs. So always be positive – even if your boss is a complete buffoon. Just say something like, "I'm very blessed to have a boss who is very good at his job", and leave it there!

The point is not only that your interviewer wants to see that you are loyal, but also that you know that they don't know the other side of the story.

Why have you been with your present employer so long?

The answer here is to avoid the implication that you were getting stale and should have moved earlier. Any answer, which contradicts this unspoken worry on the interviewer's part, is fine. For example, "I've been there for several years, but in a variety of different roles", or "The job was growing constantly, so I felt as though I was undergoing frequent changes without actually changing employer".

Why have you been with your employer for such a short time?

Your interviewer doesn't want to take on someone who is going to leave in six months. Show them that you don't really flip between jobs whatever your Resume may show. Perhaps you could answer with "I'd like to settle in one company for several years, but I've found that up to now, that I've had to move in order to widen my experience and avoid getting stale in the job"

You look like a job jumper to me.

This is much worse than the previous question. If it is not only your current or most recent employer that you've spent a short time with, but previous employers too, your interviewer will quite understandably be concerned that you'll leave them within a few months too. Nowadays people typically change jobs roughly every two to five years but anything more frequently than this looks worrying to a potential employer and some industries expect their employees to stay with them longer.

If your Resume gives the impression that you barely sit down at your desk before you're off again, you can expect this question. So how do you reassure the interviewer that this time you'd be here to stay? The last thing you want to do is to launch into a lengthy, defensive justification for each job move in turn. Far better to give a catch – all reason for moving so frequently.

So maybe you should adopt this kind of approach "I'd like to find a company I can settle down in and really make a mark. Until now I've found that I've had to change jobs in order to keep finding challenge in my work."

Why haven't you found a new job yet?

The implication behind this question is that you can't be much good if no one wants to give you a job. So, you need to indicate that it has been your choice to spend some time job – hunting. You need to give a response along the lines of "It's important that I only accept a job that seems right for me, and where I can see that I can make a contribution to the company".

If you have turned down any offers, say so: "I have had job offers, but I didn't feel the positions were right for me, and that I was right for the companies concerned".

How can you attend this interview while you are employed elsewhere?

Avoid coming across as being dishonest in any way. If you told your boss you had to stay home for the Canal plus Satellite man to call, or that you had a dentist appointment, keep quiet about it. Otherwise the interviewer knows that if they offer you the job, they'll be wondering what's going on every time you ask for time off to go to the dentists.

Ideally, your boss knows you are looking for work and is aware you are at an interview. However, in the real world this generally isn't the case. Assuming your boss actually has no idea where you are the only valid justification for taking time off here is that you took a day's holiday and you took it in order to attend this interview.

Are you talking to other organizations?

This is a great one. You want to show your prospective employer that you are in demand as it makes you a more attractive prospect. In turn if you are offered the job it can help you drive up the salary you negotiate. At the same time, if you tell them that you've had three other offers already, they may put you off if they still have a long way to go – more interviews for example. So, indicate that you are talking to others without suggesting you are on the verge of taking another job. It's not a total lie but let them know you are doing well.

What other types of jobs or organization are you applying to?

You don't need to say exactly where you've applied. Occasionally you may be asked directly where else you've applied but you can avoid answering by saying that the companies concerned haven't advertised the positions so you don't feel it is right to divulge this information. That lets you off the hook and shows your ability to keep confidence. But the interviewer can get around it with this question – asking not for names of companies but merely types of job and company. The important thing here is to show that you want this job

You may be overqualified for this job.

The worry the interviewer is revealing here is that if they offer you the job you will quickly become bored and leave. You may have reservations on this front yourself, but at this stage you should still give it your best to get the job. If you are going to turn it down do so when it's offered – you should never write it off halfway through the interview.

For the moment you are going to give the best answer you can. Say that strong, dynamic companies can always use whatever talents they have to hand. You want to stay with the company for a while and if your experience and skills are strong enough you are sure they will find a way to keep you challenged and making a full contribution.

Reassuring the Interviewer

If your interviewers have a worry about something in your application that makes them think that you may not be able to do the job what are they going to do? If they know their job they will probe until they get a satisfactory answer from you. And that's the way you want it!

If they don't ask you questions, the likely result is that they won't offer you the job. If the interviewer doesn't ask, you can't reassure them that the employment gap is no reflection on your ability to do the job.

Some interviewers find it easy to probe these areas of concern. But other are less assertive and worry that they may offend or upset you. They shouldn't because you will be grateful for the chance to reassure them. But in case your interviewer is reticent, be ready to pick up on their hints and fill them in on the facts. Otherwise both of you may address the issue full on and you could end up missing out on the job because of some unfounded worry on the interviewer's part.

What do you think about the Israeli-Gaza conflict or privatization (or a question of that nature)?

The idea behind this question is to see if you take an interest in what goes on in the world in general and it also gives them an insight into your values and attitudes to life. Politically correct answers aren't always the right ones, what you need to do is demonstrate that you have the ability to see both sides of an issue, that you don't see things in an over simplistic way and that you have the ability to discuss a subject properly and are capable of making a calculated judgment. What you don't want to do is rant on about your political views without acknowledging both sides of the debate.

This question can be particularly relevant to certain industries, if for example you work for a bank you might be asked your views on interest rates, or a chemical company may ask your views on global warming etc. If you have done your research on the company you may have an insight into what type of answer is needed here.

So, you'll want to know which type of questions to ask that will give a good impression and which type not to ask so that the interviewer will not be put off. Let's start with the questions you don't want to ask;

- Will I get my own office?
- What holiday entitlement do I get?
- Do I get paid if I'm off sick?
- I go out Wednesday nights and have a few beers with my mates, is it OK to come in at 10 am on a Thursday?
- How much do I earn and do I get a Christmas bonus?
- How long do I get for lunch?
- Do I get a choice of company car?

You can see from this list that these questions are aimed at what you get out of this company, not what benefits you can offer to them. Of course, all of these questions are relevant to you but as yet you haven't been offered the job so now is not a good time to discuss them. Should you be offered the job there will be plenty of time to negotiate all of these.

There are many questions you will want to ask that show your enthusiasm towards the company and the job they are offering which will compliment what you are able to contribute to them. Asked correctly, they will make you look ambitious, intelligent and committed so it is important that you give this your very best.

The easiest thing to do is to compile a list of brief questions. If you think you will forget them right them down on your notepad. The interviewer will not mind you getting this out of your briefcase.

Remember, the interview is not over yet so don't feel that you can sit back and relax. The questions you do and don't ask here say a great deal about you and will still influence any decision about whether you will be offered the job. It would be fatal not to ask any questions at all, first because it looks unenthusiastic and makes you look like you are not really interested in the position and second because there will definitely be questions that the interviewer has not covered and you will want to answers to for your own peace of mind. After all, if you change jobs you want to make sure that you know as much as possible about the job you are moving to, this is a major decision in your career.

What do you think are the key trends in this industry?

This question won't be difficult to answer as long as you've done your homework and research – which is the point of the question and an area that the interviewer wants to establish. This question is really an advanced version of "What do you know about our company?" So, the important thing here is to make sure you do your homework properly and identify the key industry trends, ready to impress the interviewer.

Even if you're applying for a job in the industry you already work in you should still prepare an answer to this question. It won't necessarily come to you, clearly and instinctively, in the heat of the moment.

What is your present boss's greatest weakness?

"Where would you like me to start" is the true and honest answer, but not the right one! This question really invites you to drop yourself in it. Don't fall for it, no matter how long the list of faults – remember "LOYALTY", your interviewer could soon be your new boss and he wants to think that you will always speak nicely about him.

You could answer this question along the lines of "To be honest, I'm lucky to have a very supportive boss who is good at his job and very easy to get on with."

How do you evaluate your present company?

They are a great company that have taught you a lot and offered you plenty of opportunity and provided you with excellent training to enable you to do the job to the best of your ability. You have just outgrown them. This is the correct statement to make regardless of what you and your colleagues really think.

What is your management style?

Make sure that your answer to this question is relevant and don't try and give a textbook answer. You can make your point in a couple of sentences such as "I believe you have to be firm with your team but you also have to treat them with a fair approach."

Are you a good manager?

What a silly question – of course you are! The answer is always "Yes." This question follows the one from above and if you haven't already been asked about your management style you can add this to your answer. Your answer could be "Yes I am. I prefer a carrot rather than a stick approach and I am a great believer in being firm with my team but at the same time being fair".

Are you a natural leader?

You are only likely to be asked this question if the job you are applying for involves some form of management or leadership. The answer to this must be positive and it doesn't have to relate purely to work. Make sure you give an example of your leadership qualities.

How do you work in a team?

This is another question you need to answer honestly, but pick a relevant way to express your teamwork style. Give a fairly brief answer, such as "I enjoy being part of a team, and I like the flexibility that it demands. I get a real pleasure out of collective success". Follow your remarks up with an example of what you mean. If teamwork is going to be an important part of the job you are applying for you should certainly expect this question to come up so make sure you have your answer ready.

How creative are you?

If you are applying for a job, which has a creative role, you are likely to be asked this question. Be ready with your answers. Give examples of how you use any creative techniques you may have which will show that you take your creativity seriously.

How do you get the best from people?

If you are applying for a management role it is highly likely you'll be asked this question. The kind of skills that interviewers like to hear about is:

- Good communication skills
- Teamwork
- Recognizing each person as an individual
- Setting a sound and good example
- Praising good performances.

How do you resolve conflict in your team?

You need to answer this question honestly. Find an example of conflict that you have had in your own team and use this to demonstrate your diplomatic abilities. The kinds of skills you need to demonstrate are:

- Fairness
- Addressing problems with individuals privately
- Making sure you get to the root of the problem
- Finding a solution that the persons concerned are willing to adhere to.

When would you expect a promotion?

You shouldn't give a firm timescale on this. The answer is, you should expect a promotion when you deserve it. "I would hope to be promoted once I have demonstrated my value to the company and shown that I am worth it."

And show how this job suits your long term aims: "That's why I want to join a large organization so there are plenty of opportunities when I've gained the skills and experience."

What is your present salary?

This question is a bit tricky and you may want to give a non-committal answer. If you go straight in with "I earn $ 100,000 plus benefits and an AUDI A6 SPORT and free weekend tickets to the Philadelphia Union games" should you be offered the job they will offer you as close to this as your present package. Then ask if you can return the question later once you get to a point where you need to talk about it in more detail.

What salary are you expecting?

Again, another tricky one which, ideally, you don't want to be too committal over. If you commit to a salary at this stage you won't be able to negotiate later and if you ask for too much, you'll scare them off. So here it would be good to answer with another question so try something like "What salary would you be expecting to pay for this position?" or ask what salary range has been given for this position. If the interviewer doesn't want to divulge this then it's not unreasonable for you to decline to answer too. Should the interviewer quote a salary and ask for your response let them know you were thinking of something a little higher – but remember don't make it out of their reach

How much do you think you're worth?

Salary questions usually speak good news. After all, why bother start-discussing salaries if they weren't even considering offering you the job? This question is really the above question re – worded. It should be answered in the same way as the above question – once you've played the previous game of making them go first it's just a case of justifying what you're asking for.

The chances are that you will already have a good idea of what the going rate for the job is in the industry, so ask for a little more and explain that you've studied salary surveys and so on. Since your experience is above average for the job you believe that you're worth above average pay. As a point of interest generally the interviewer will state that the amount you have asked for is too much – generally speaking it's just a tactic don't let them knock your confidence.

Salary Variables

Variables are all of the other factors that are not necessarily salary orientated. They are things such as holiday entitlement, luncheon vouchers or expenses, performance related bonuses, commission, overtime, profit sharing, private health insurance, share options, childcare contribution, sports/gym facilities, company car, mobile phone, rail or travel ticket and non-contributory pension. This list is not exhaustive and it would be fairly unrealistic to ask for all of these benefits, the best thing to do is choose maybe two or three and see how you get on.

Deal Negotiating

Now let's get down to real business! It's always wise to leave salary negotiation and any benefits package until you've been offered the job. The reason being that once the employer has decided that you're the employee for them, you are in a much stronger position to negotiate. Deal negotiating is not just about money and benefits; it's about negotiating the whole contract. This gives the perception that you know what you are worth and that you are not prepared to settle for less.

This might not be exactly what your employer wants, but it will show that you have good negotiating qualities and it is likely that you will apply these to the job – it's a good quality to have. There's no point in trying to squeeze them like a lemon, at the end of the day they can only pay you what they can afford and you might end up losing the job at the last minute – something you won't want to do because of greed. Unless you aren't prepared to take the job under a certain salary level you need to make sure you ask them what they can afford, so how much can they afford.

- If a salary range has been advertised or quoted to you can reasonably expect to get the top end of the range as long as you can demonstrate you are worth it.
- If an approximate salary has been quoted you have for sure about 10% leeway.
- If the position is one where the salary is in a set pay scale where there is no flexibility you can always negotiate with the benefits package.

Remember that the more valuable you can demonstrate that you are the better chance you will have of negotiating a higher salary. So how do you prove this? Your qualifications are always a good start. If you have more qualifications than were originally advertised for the position then that's a plus point. You will definitely need to prepare some justifications for asking top dollar.

At the end of the day you have been offered the job because the employer thinks that you can bring more to the table than any of the other candidates so you presumably have above average qualities, all you need to do is identify them and then use them in your negotiating techniques.

DON'T GIVE AWAY FREE CONCESSIONS

This is a crucial rule when negotiating. If you are asked to accept a lower salary or agree that you will start on a lower salary and then in six months be given an increase to the level you have requested then **don't give this concession for free**. You can accept this but you want them to make a concession on their part such as;

- "We can offer you a salary review in six months" You can accept this but only on the basis that your salary increases by at least 20% for example when your probation is up.
- "Our standard holiday entitlement is three weeks and we can't extend that" Fine OK but if that's the case I would need at least five days a year leave for personal reasons.

You know where we are going with this! The idea is that if you have to give something away, you should gain something in its place. BUSINESS 101, REALLY.

Get All Your Cards on the Table

If you are dealing with a hardball manager who is keen to get the very best deal, they can for their company it can be quite tricky. There is a guarantee that they will hold a card up their sleeve and you need to find out exactly what it is. It may be that they have concessions that they want you to agree before they will agree to a certain salary or benefit. It might be that they want you to start on a lower salary or maybe take on additional tasks not specified in the job description in addition to the normal job.

Generally speaking, this is a bit underhanded and ruthless and the chances are they will spring it on you at the last minute when you have pretty much agreed on the salary.

All is not lost, however. You can prevent this situation from happening by laying down your cards from the start. You can say "We need to talk about my salary and holiday entitlement. Are there any other issues we need to discuss at the same time?" You have now made it extremely difficult for your employer to not mention the facts.

Bad Timing

Life is complicated. The problem is when you have been offered a job but you're waiting to hear from another job, which you think is better. You don't want to accept the first job and then find out a couple of days later that you've been offered the second one too it would be a disaster.

There are a couple of ways to solve this problem. The first one would be to contact the employer and tell them that you'd like 24 hours to decide. This isn't unreasonable and as long as you keep the time extension short, they won't think anything of it. No one wants to play second best and if they think you're looking for a better offer with another company you could blow your chances.

Now you are in the driving seat! The second idea would be to contact the company whose decision you are waiting on and explain to them the situation. Chances are they will be glad to hear that they are your first choice and it always looks good if everyone wants to employ you and that you are in demand. It's unlikely that they will give you an answer right away, but it may be that they will get back to you the following day with their answer – it really doesn't matter if it's "no," because all of your doors are open!

It isn't a good idea to use this technique if you haven't been offered a job (although it seems tempting) because the end result is that if it was a tossup between you and another candidate they may well choose the other candidate due to the time restrictions you are placing on them – you don't want to lose the chances of getting this job by being overzealous if time is just a matter of course.

Interviewing at Institutions of Higher Learning

Ethical Principles of College Recruiting for Candidates

The Office of Career Services and the National Association of Colleges and Employers expect students to adhere to the following principles of college recruiting:

- In seeking interviews, you should recognize your responsibility to analyze your values, interests and abilities, and consider carefully your employment objectives and appropriate ways of meeting them. You should read available literature, consult other sources for information about the employer, and organize your thoughts in order that you may intelligently ask and answer questions.
- You should contact Career Services well in advance regarding desired interviews or cancellations.
- You should use care in filling out forms that may be requested in preparation for the interview.
- In your interview, you should recognize that you are representing your college, as well as yourself, and you should be punctual and professional in your conduct.
- You should promptly acknowledge an invitation to visit an employer's premises. You should accept an invitation only when you are sincerely interested in exploring employment.
- When you are invited to visit an employer's location at the employer's expense, an accurate record of actual expenses incurred should be kept. The actual expense pertaining to the trip should be the only expenses reported on the expense report. If two or more employers are visited on the same trip, expenses should be prorated among them.
- As soon as you determine that you will not accept an offer, you should immediately notify the employer.
- You should not continue to present yourself for interviews after accepting an employment offer.
- Your acceptance of an employment offer should be made in good faith and with the sincere intention of honoring the employment commitment.

Questions for the College Student to Ask the Employer

- What will be expected of the person who is hired for this particular position?
- Would you tell me in detail about the responsibilities of this position?
- How does this job fit into the overall structure of the department?
- What are the typical career paths for people who start in this position? What qualities are you looking for in candidates for this position?
- Is this a new position?
- How will training be conducted?
- Would you tell me about the work environment?
- How is job performance evaluated?
- Is there anything else I can tell you about my qualifications?
- I hope that I am one of the candidates you are considering. When can I expect to hear from you?

Why has this vacancy arisen?

There's nothing wrong with this question. It may have already been covered earlier on in the interview. If it hasn't, then you should ask it now. Vacancies arise all the time for various reasons, but if you get a non-committal answer from the interviewer it could mean that something controversial has happened.

Do you promote internally where possible?

If you're asking questions surrounding promotion it's fair to say that it shows you're keen to progress within this organization. You could also if interested enquire as to whether any overseas opportunities ever come up within the company as you would be willing to travel in the future for the right promotion and are flexible.

What opportunities do you offer to gain extra training, qualifications or experience?

Be a little careful about asking this question if you have already made yourself to be an expert in your field. It shows again that you are committed to your employer and the profession and that you want to do the best for your company.

If I were offered this job, where would you see me in five years?

This is a great one because it is asking your interviewer to imagine that you're in the job. This question also gives the impression of a long terms commitment to the company implying that you would want to progress. The answer, of course, will give you a greater insight into how quickly people move up through the ranks in this company. You will want to know this when considering your long-term options should you be offered the job.

Where does the company aim to be in five years?

You want to know the answer to this question for your own benefit. However, you will impress your interviewer with this as it shows that you have an interest in the benefit of the company as a whole long term and not just in your own job role.

Do you have any reservations about my ability to do this job?

You can use this statement in a broader term and it must be used in a confident manner. At the end of the day you're a salesperson and you are selling yourself as the perfect candidate for the job, this gives the interviewer a chance to clarify any points he may have, he can only say "no" if he has doesn't have any reservations. You are convincing him that you are the right person for the job if he has no reasons not to hire you.

When can I expect to hear from you?

The interviewer prior to asking you if you had any questions could have already covered this. If not, you should ask it. This is great because if they haven't responded to you by the date given it gives you a chance to contact them.

DO NOT ask the Following

- Questions that will put the interviewer on the spot. *Example: "How are women and minorities treated here?"*

- Questions that broadcast you have not done your homework. *Example: "What product does this company make?"*

- Questions that tip the interviewer off to a problem you might have. *Example: "Are people in your department easy to get along with?"*

- Questions that imply you already have the job. *Example: "Will you show me my office?"*

- Questions that cause the interviewer to wonder about your priorities. *Example: "How much money will I make? 6. How much vacation will I get?*

Final Thoughts

So, here we are. I trust you read the entire guide, or at least the parts that most interested you. I have no pithy comments or quotes of deep reflection. I'll keep my final thoughts short and sweet:

Godspeed to you and Happy job-hunting!

Check our website for more e-books and other offers:

https://www.akansonpr.com